ZOO

ZOO

OGDEN · NASH'S
ZOO

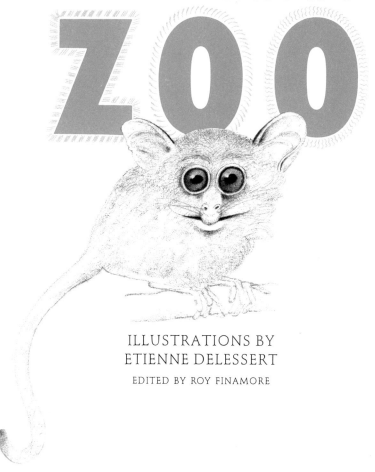

ILLUSTRATIONS BY
ETIENNE DELESSERT

EDITED BY ROY FINAMORE

STEWART, TABORI & CHANG
NEW YORK

Many of these poems first appeared in the following magazines:
The New Yorker, Saturday Evening Post, Signature, and *Travel & Camera.*

Illustrations copyright © 1987 by Etienne Delessert.

Published in 1987 by Stewart, Tabori & Chang, Inc.,
740 Broadway, New York, New York 10003.

Library of Congress Cataloging-in-Publication Data

Nash, Ogden, 1902–1971.
  Ogden Nash's zoo.

  1. Animals—Poetry. I. Delessert, Etienne.
II. Finamore, Roy. III. Title. IV. Title: Zoo.
PS3527.A637Z4 1987   811'.52   86-23173
ISBN 0-941434-95-8

Distributed by Workman Publishing,
1 West 39 Street, New York, New York 10018.
Printed in Japan

87 88 89 90 10 9 8 7 6 5 4 3 2 1

CONTENTS

CHAPTER 1

THE CAT IS OUT

THE CAT

You get a wife, you get a house,

Eventually you get a mouse.

You get some words regarding mice,

You get a kitty in a trice.

By two A.M., or thereabout,

The mouse is in, the cat is out.

It dawns upon you, in your cot,

The mouse is silent, the cat is not.

Instead of Pussy, says your spouse,

You should have bought another mouse.

THE DOG

The truth I do not stretch or shove

When I state the dog is full of love.

I've also proved, by actual test,

A wet dog is the lovingest.

Here's a verse about rabbits

That doesn't mention their habits.

THE  QUIRREL

A squirrel to some is a squirrel,

To others, a squirrel's a squirl.

Since freedom of speech is the birthright of each,

I can only this fable unfurl:

A virile young squirrel named Cyril,

In an argument over a girl,

Was lambasted from here to the Tyrol

By a churl of a squirl named Earl.

CHAPTER 2

SCRAM, LAMB

Behold the duck.

It does not cluck.

A cluck it lacks.

It quacks.

It is specially fond

Of a puddle or pond.

When it dines or sups,

It bottoms ups.

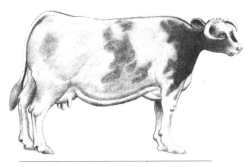

The cow is of the bovine ilk;

One end is moo, the other, milk.

THE TURKEY

There is nothing more perky

Than a masculine turkey.

When he struts he struts

With no ifs or buts.

When his face is apoplectic

His harem grows hectic,

And when he gobbles

Their universe wobbles.

THE POULTRIES

Let's think of eggs.

They have no legs.

Chickens come from eggs

But they have legs.

The plot thickens;

Eggs come from chickens,

But have no legs under 'em.

What a conundrum!

THE MULES

In the world of mules

There are no rules.

THE LAMB

Little gamboling lamb,

Do you know where you am?

In a patch of mint.

I'll give you a hint.

Scram,

Lamb!

CHAPTER 3

THE AQUARIUM

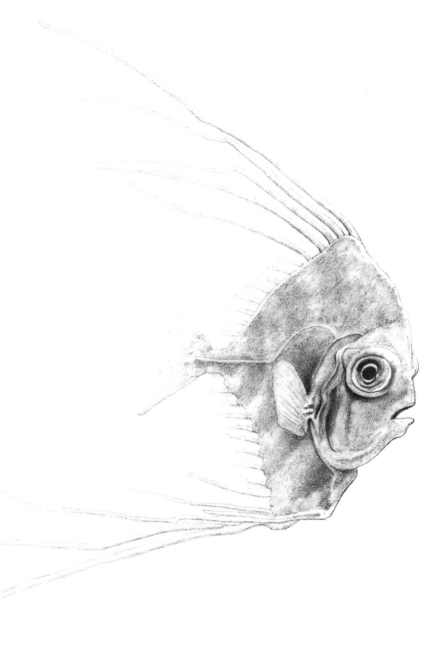

Some fish are minnows,

Some are whales.

People like dimples,

Fish like scales.

Some fish are slim,

And some are round.

Fish don't get cold,

And don't get drowned.

But every fish wife

Is jealous for her fish

Of what we call mermaids,

And they call merfish.

THE UPPY

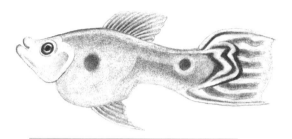

Whales have calves,

Cats have kittens,

Bears have cubs,

Bats have bittens.

Swans have cygnets,

Seals have puppies,

But guppies just have little guppies.

THE TORTOISE

Come crown my brows with leaves of myrtle;

I know the tortoise is a turtle.

Come carve my name in stone immortal;

I know the turtoise is a tortle;

I know to my profound despair;

I bet on one to beat a hare.

I also know I'm now a pauper

Because of its tortley turtley torpor.

THE LAMPREY

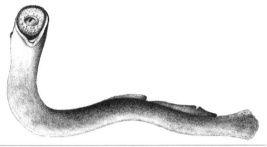

Lampreys are hagfish. In that one word I've said it.

I only know one item to their credit.

The early English had good cause to love them;

Wicked King John died from a surfeit of them.

THE PORPOISE

I kind of like the playful porpoise,

A healthy mind in a healthy corpus.

He and his cousin, the playful dolphin,

Why they like swimmin like I like golphin.

THE EEL

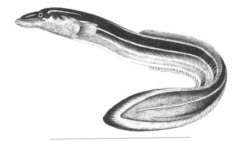

I don't mind eels

Except as meals.

And the way they feels.

THE SHRIMP

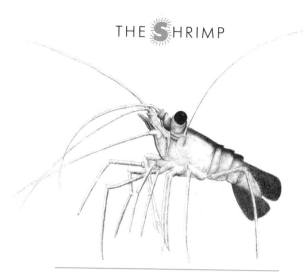

A shrimp who sought his lady shrimp

Could catch no glimpse,

Not even a glimp.

At times, translucence

Is rather a nuisance.

THE HARK

How many Scientists have written

The shark is gentle as a kitten!

Yet this I know about the shark:

His bite is worser than his bark.

THE SQUID

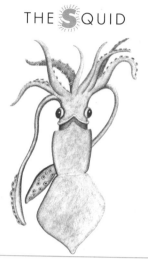

What happy appellations these

Of birds and beasts in companies!

A shrewdness of apes, a sloth of bears,

A soulk of foxes, a huske of hares.

An exaltation 'tis of larks,

And possibly a grin of sharks,

But I declare a squirt of squid

I should not like to be amid,

Though bachelors claim that a cloud of sepia

Makes a splendid hiding place in Leap Year.

THE 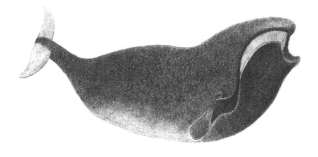HALE

Behold the sulphur-bottom whale,

Some 25 yards from nose to tail.

I find it somewhat ludicrous

That whales are mammals, just like us,

And basking where the plankton teems

They dream their sweet cetacean dreams.

One dreaming sulphur-bottom chick

In her Maidenform bra met Moby-Dick.

The clam, esteemed by gourmets highly,

Is said to live the life of Riley;

When you are lolling on a piazza

It's what you are as happy as a.

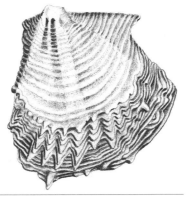

The oyster's a confusing suitor;

It's masc., and fem., and even neuter.

At times it wonders, may what come,

Am I husband, wife, or chum.

CHAPTER 4

CREEPS AND CRAWLS

The Lord in His wisdom made the fly

And then forgot to tell us why.

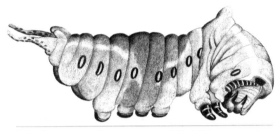

I find among the poems of Schiller

No mention of the caterpillar,

Nor can I find one anywhere

In Petrarch or in Baudelaire,

So here I sit in extra session

To give my personal impression.

The caterpillar, as it's called,

Is often hairy, seldom bald;

It looks as if it never shaves;

When as it walks, it walks in waves;

And from the cradle to the chrysalis

It's utterly speechless, songless, whistleless.

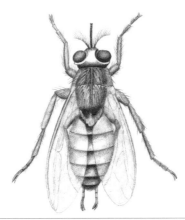

Aunt Betsy was fixing to change her will,

And would have left us out in the chill.

A *Glossina morsitans* bit Aunt Betsy.

Tsk tsk, tsetse.

THE ANT

The ant has made himself illustrious

Through constant industry industrious.

So what?

Would you be calm and placid

If you were full of formic acid?

THE PRAYING MANTIS

From whence arrived the praying mantis?

From outer space, or lost Atlantis?

I glimpse the grim, green metal mug

That masks this pseudo-saintly bug,

Orthopterous, also carnivorous,

And faintly whisper, Lord deliver us.

THE CENTIPEDE

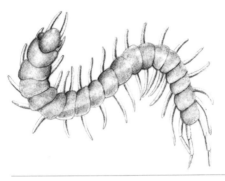

I objurgate the centipede,

A bug we do not really need.

At sleepy-time he beats a path

Straight to the bedroom or the bath.

You always wallop where he's not,

Or, if he is, he makes a spot.

THE TERMITE

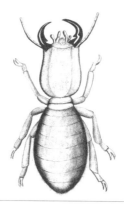

Some primal termite knocked on wood

And tasted it, and found it good,

And that is why your Cousin May

Fell through the parlor floor today.

THE FIREFLY

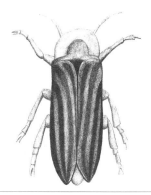

The firefly's flame

Is something for which science has no name.

I can think of nothing eerier

Than flying around with an unidentified glow

    on a person's posterior.

ARE INCURABLY
PHILHARMONIC

THE BIRDS

Puccini was Latin, and Wagner Teutonic,

And birds are incurably philharmonic.

Suburban yards and rural vistas

Are filled with avian Andrews Sisters.

The skylark sings a roundelay,

The crow sings "The Road to Mandalay,"

The nightingale sings a lullaby

And the sea gull sings a gullaby.

That's what shepherds listened to in Arcadia

Before somebody invented the radia.

THE CANARY

The song of canaries

Never varies,

And when they're moulting

They're pretty revolting.

THE CUCKOO

Cuckoos lead Bohemian lives.

They fail as husbands and as wives.

Therefore they cynically disparage

Everybody else's marriage.

The grackle's voice is less than mellow,

His heart is black, his eye is yellow,

He bullies more attractive birds

With hoodlum deeds and vulgar words,

And should a human interfere,

Attacks that human in the rear.

I cannot help but deem the grackle

An ornithological debacle.

THE OSTRICH

The ostrich roams the great Sahara.

Its mouth is wide, its neck is narra.

It has such long and lofty legs,

I'm glad it sits to lay its eggs.

THE STORK

From long descriptions I have heard

I guess this creature is a bird.

I've nothing else of him to say,

Except I wish he'd go away.

THE SWAN

Scholars call the masculine swan a cob;

I call him a narcissistic snob.

He looks in the mirror over and over,

And claims to have never heard of Pavlova.

The toucan's profile is prognathous,

Its person is a thing of bathos.

If even I can tell a toucan

I'm reasonably sure that you can.

CHAPTER 6

TEASE THE COBRA

Whenever I behold an asp

I can't suppress a startled gasp.

I do not charge the asp with matricide,

But what about his Cleopatricide?

THE OBRA

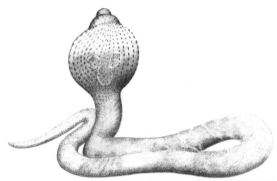

This creature fills its mouth with venum

And walks upon its duodenum.

He who attempts to tease the cobra

Is soon a sadder he, and sobra.

THE PYTHON

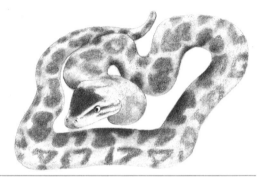

The python has, and I fib no fibs,

318 pairs of ribs.

In stating this I place reliance

On a seance with one who died for science.

This figure is sworn to and attested;

He counted them while being digested.

THE SKINK

Let us do justice to the skink

Who isn't what so many think.

On consultation with a wizard

I find the skink a kind of lizard.

Since he is not a printer's whim,

Don't sniff and back away from him,

Or you may be adjudged too drunk

To tell a lizard from a skunk.

CHAPTER 7

BEHOLD THE
HIPPOPOTAMUS

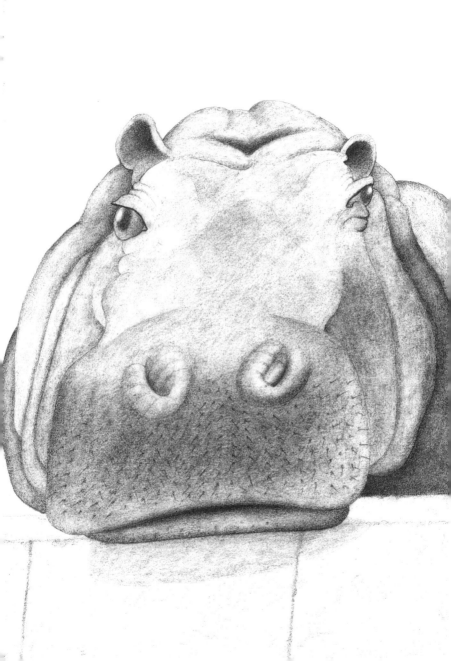

THE  AMEL

The camel has a single hump;

The dromedary, two;

Or else the other way around.

I'm never sure. Are you?

THE LK

Moose makes me think of caribou,

And caribou, of moose,

With, even from their point of view,

Legitimate excuse.

Why then, when I behold an elk,

Can I but think of Lawrence Welk?

THE HIPPOPOTAMUS

Behold the hippopotamus!

We laugh at how he looks to us,

And yet in moments dank and grim

I wonder how we look to him.

Peace, peace, thou hippopotamus!

We really look all right to us,

As you no doubt delight the eye

Of other hippopotami.

THE LAMA

The one-l lama,

He's a priest.

The two-l llama,

He's a beast.

And I will bet

A silk pajama

There isn't any

Three-l lllama.*

*The author's attention has been called
to a type of conflagration known as a
three-alarmer. Pooh.

THE LION

Oh, weep for Mr. and Mrs. Bryan!

He was eaten by a lion;

Following which, the lion's lioness

Up and swallowed Bryan's Bryaness.

MANHATTAN MONKEY

The monkey is

A child of whim;

Ethics mean nothing

Much to him;

His life is full

Of fun and zest;

He turns his critics

With a jest;

A tailor and

A friend or two

Could make him Mayor

Of the zoo.

THE PANDA

I love the Baby Giant Panda;

I'd welcome one to my veranda.

I never worry, wondering maybe

Whether it isn't Giant Baby;

I leave such matters to the scientists:

The Giant Baby—and Baby Giantists.

I simply wish a julep and a

Giant Baby Giant Panda.

THE PANTHER

The panther is like a leopard,

Except it hasn't been peppered.

Should you behold a panther crouch,

Prepare to say Ouch.

Better yet, if called by a panther,

Don't anther.

THE SHREW

Strange as it seems, the smallest mammal

Is the shrew, and not the camel.

And that is all I ever knew,

Or wish to know, about the shrew.

THE **R**HINOCEROS

The rhino is a homely beast,

For human eyes he's not a feast.

Farewell, farewell, you old rhinoceros,

I'll stare at something less prepoceros.

THE ANGAROO

O Kangaroo, O Kangaroo,

Be grateful that you're in the zoo,

And not transmuted by a boomerang

To zestful tangy Kangaroo meringue.

THE ARMADILLO

The armadillo lives inside

A corrugated plated hide.

Below the border this useful creature

Of tidy kitchens is a feature,

For housewives use an armadillo

To scour their pots, instead of Brillo.

CHAPTER 8

DID NOT CREATE IT

THE G RYNCH

I dearly love the three-toed grynch,

It grows upon me inch by inch.

Each home with one should be provided;

The Lord did not create it, so I did.

It's useful for closing conversations

With stubborn salesmen and poor relations.

Long-winded storytellers flinch

If I bring up the three-toed grynch.

When I speak of the grynch which I adore

I'm a bore, I'm a bore, I'm a fabulous bore.

But so can life be; in a pinch,

I recommend the three-toed grynch.

THE PHOENIX

Deep in the study

Of eugenics

We find that fabled

Fowl, the Phoenix.

The wisest bird

As ever was,

Rejecting other

Mas and Pas,

It lays one egg,

Not ten or twelve,

And when it's hatched,

Out pops itselve.

DESIGNED BY RITA MARSHALL

COMPOSED IN STEMPEL SCHNEIDLER LIGHT
AND FUTURA EXTRA BLACK CONDENSED
BY TRUFONT TYPOGRAPHERS, INC.,
HICKSVILLE, NEW YORK.

PRINTED AND BOUND BY
TOPPAN PRINTING COMPANY, LTD.,
TOKYO, JAPAN.